THIS OVERFLOWING LIGHT

Books by Janine Beichman

Masaoka Shiki: His Life and Works (Cheng & Tsui, 2002)
Embracing the Firebird: Yosano Akiko and the Birth of the Female Voice in Modern Japanese Poetry (University of Hawaii Press, 2002)

TRANSLATIONS

Harumi (Jakuchō) Setouchi, *The End of Summer* (Kodansha International, 1989)
Makoto Ōoka, *A Poet's Anthology: The Range of Japanese Poetry* (Katydid Books, 1994)
Makoto Ōoka, *Poems for All Seasons: An Anthology of Japanese Poetry from Ancient Times to the Present* (Kodansha International, 2002)
Abbess Kasanoin Jikun, *In Iris Fields: Remembrances and Poetry* (Tankosha, 2009; with Ann Cary)
Makoto Ōoka, *Beneath the Sleepless Tossing of the Planets: Selected Poems 1972–1989* (Kurodahan Press, 2018)
Minoru Ozawa, *Well-Versed: Exploring Modern Japanese Haiku* (Japan Publishing Industry Foundation for Culture, 2021)
Koka Fukushima, *Koka: A Passion for Ikebana* (Koka Fukushima, 2021)

PLAY

Drifting Fires: An American Nō (Shichigatsudō Press, 1986)

THIS OVERFLOWING LIGHT

SELECTED POEMS

RIN ISHIGAKI

Rin Ishigaki

Selected, translated, and with an introduction and notes by

JANINE BEICHMAN

ISOBAR PRESS

First published in 2022 by

Isobar Press
Sakura 2-21-23-202, Setagaya-ku,
Tokyo 156-0053, Japan
&
14 Isokon Flats, Lawn Road,
London NW3 2XD, United Kingdom

https://isobarpress.com

ISBN 978-4-907359-41-6

Translations, introduction
and notes © Janine Beichman, 2022

All rights reserved.

No part of this publication may be reproduced in whole or in part, or stored in a retrieval system, or transmitted in any form or by any means, electronic, mechanical, photocopying, recording, or otherwise, without the prior written permission of the copyright holder, with the exception of short quotations for review or illustrative purposes.

Some of these translations first appeared in slightly different form in *The Columbia Anthology of Modern Japanese Literature* and *Across Time and Genre: Reading and Writing Women's Texts,* in the journal *Literary Imagination,* and online in *Trends in Japan* and *Nippon.com.*

For Takeo

Ishigaki Rin, March 9, 1990, age 70.
Courtesy of the Minamiizu-chō Public Library.

Contents

List of Illustrations	10
A Note on Japanese Names	10
Acknowledgements	11
Bibliographical Note	12
Introduction	15

from *Before Me the Soup Pot the Rice Pot and the Bright Burning Flame* (Watashi no mae ni aru nabe to okama to moeru hi to, 1959)

Greetings	43
An Evening Tale	45
In a Hundred Human Bellies	47
Before Me the Soup Pot the Rice Pot and the Bright Burning Flame	48
The Women's Bath	50
There Is in This World	52
The Watcher	53
0	54
The Sea and Apples	56
Roof	57
Poverty	59
The Pay Envelope	60
Getting Ready	62
These Days I	63
Secret	64
This Overflowing Light	65
The Shoes That Fell Off	66

from *Nameplates and More* (Hyōsatsu nado, 1968)

Little Clams	69
Nameplates	70
Living	71
Traveling On	72
Flowers	73
Island	74
Cliff	75
Rakugo	76
Festival of the Blind	78
Seascape	80
Kappa Heaven	82
The Runaway's Song	83
Nursery Rhyme	85
Sprouting	86

from *My Life in Brief* (Ryakureki, 1979)

The Rite	91
The Book of the Dead	92
Yesterday's Faces	93
My Life in Brief	94
Tree	95
The Twilight Crane	96
Customs	97
After the Ceremony	98
Woman	99
Lullaby	100

from *Tender Words* (Yasashii Kotoba, 1984)

Sweetfish   103

Uncollected

Goodnight   107

Notes to the Poems   111

Original Poem Titles   117

List of Illustrations

Front cover: New Year card for 1964, the Year of the Dragon, hand-made by Ishigaki Rin.

Title page: Ishigaki Rin's signature.

Page 6: Ishigaki Rin, March 9, 1990, age 70.

Page 30: Ishigaki Rin with her brother Ishigaki Toshiharu, a few weeks before her death in 2004.

Page 40: The Industrial Bank of Japan in the 1950s.

Page 64: Manuscript of *Himegoto* (Secret).

Page 68: Manuscript of *Shijimi* (Little Clams).

Page 90: Ishigaki Rin, September 22, 1959, age 39, on the roof of the Industrial Bank of Japan, wearing her employee's uniform.

Page 102: Ishigaki Rin, 1939, age 19.

Page 104: Ishigaki Rin, 1937, age 17.

All illustrations are courtesy of the Minamiizu-chō Public Library except for Ishigaki Rin's signature on the title page, which is in the collection of the translator, and the photograph of the Industrial Bank of Japan, which is in the public domain.

A Note on Japanese Names

Throughout this book Japanese names are printed in the customary Japanese order with family names first, except in the case of Japanese authors who mostly publish in English, and of Ishigaki Rin, whose name on the cover and the title page is printed in the English-language order for the convenience of booksellers and librarians.

Acknowledgements

Three people were essential to this project: Ōoka Makoto, who first suggested it, Ishigaki Rin, who gave it her blessing, and Paul Rossiter, who has given it a home at Isobar Press as both editor and publisher. I am deeply grateful to them all, as well as to the Minamiizu-chō Board of Education for kindly facilitating permission to use the photographs of Ishigaki Rin, her handwritten manuscripts, and her handmade New Year's card. I also remember with pleasure and gratitude the kindness of those who gave me aid and encouragement along the way: Jeffrey Angles, Tomoko Aoyama, Phyllis Birnbaum, John Einarsen, Sarah Frederick, Alisa Freedman, Fukase Saki (Ōoka Kaneko), Takako Lento, Etsuko Morimura, Nancy Ross, M.W. Shores, John Solt, Itsuki Takebayashi, Rosanna Warren, Kay Watanabe, Takeo Yamamoto, and Yasuhiro Yotsumoto.

Bibliographic Note

During her lifetime, Ishigaki Rin published four books of poetry and three of essays, as well as two poetry anthologies with commentary. These are listed below in chronological order of publication and were my sources for the poems in this book and the essays cited in my introduction and notes. In all cases, the place of publication is Tokyo and the author is Ishigaki Rin.

Except for the two anthologies, all Ishigaki's works are available in more than one edition, most of them fortunately virtually uniform. Here only the first editions are listed. The page numbers in the notes to my introduction, for excerpts from the essay collections, refer to the later Chikuma Bunko series editions (see page 36 for details).

As of this writing, there is no complete works, but the four collections of poetry published during Ishigaki's lifetime were reprinted by Kashinsha in 1987–89 in four volumes, under the title *Ishigaki Rin Bunko*.

There is in addition a posthumous collection, *Remon to Nezumi* (The lemon and the mouse), published by Dōwaya in 2008, which includes a portion of the uncollected poems left behind when Ishigaki died.

There are as well a number of editions of Ishigaki's 'selected poems,' a recent one being *Ishigaki Rin Shishū* (Iwanami Bunko 200-1, Iwanami Shoten, 2016), edited and with an afterword by the poet Ito Hiromi.

For English-language literary criticism about Ishigaki, see Aoyama, Tomoko, 'Food, Humor, and Gender in Ishigaki Rin's Poetry,' in Gitanjali G. Shahani, ed., *Food and Literature*, Cambridge: Cambridge University Press, 2018, 303–318. https://doi.org/10.1017/9781108661492.017

POEMS

Watashi no mae ni aru nabe to okama to moeru hi to ((Before me the soup pot the rice pot and the bright burning flame). Shoshi Yuriika, 1959.
Hyōsatsu nado (Nameplates and more). Shichōsha, 1968.
Ryakureki (My life in brief). Kashinsha, 1979.
Yasashii Kotoba (Tender words). Kashinsha, 1984.

ESSAYS

Yūmoa no sakoku (Humor's forbidden country). Hokuyōsha, 1973.
Honō ni te wo kazashite (Warming my hands at the flame). Chikuma Shobō, 1980.
Yoru no taiko (Night drum). Chikuma Shobō, 1989.

ANTHOLOGIES

Shi no okurimono 3 Katei no shi (The gifts of poetry 3, Poems of the home). Chikuma Shobō, 1981.
Shi no naka no fūkei (The inner landscapes of poetry). Fujin-no-tomo-sha, 1992.

In the introduction and notes, I use the following abbreviations for Ishigaki's essay collections:

Sakoku   *Yūmoa no sakoku*
Honō   *Honō ni te wo kazashite*
Taiko   *Yoru no taiko*

There was only one thing I did because I wanted to do it, a space where I could do as I pleased, and that was poetry....

Words have the power to bring people infinite riches. Fortunately, they do not obey the rules of private property, so this power is accessible to everyone. No one has to pay for the right to use the personal pronoun 'I.' That, I think, is an excellent thing.

– Ishigaki Rin
'To write poetry and to live,' *Humor's Forbidden Country*

Introduction[1]

Ishigaki Rin never married, a radical choice for a woman of her time and place. When she was in her early thirties, she asked her beloved grandfather, who had lived with her family from before she was born, what he thought of a woman who was getting on in years living on her own:

- Do you think I can get along without marrying?
- Yes, of course.
- Actually, I'm thinking of being the last in our line.
- Well, I think that's just fine. It's not easy to be happy when you're human.

Then he recited for me the poem about departing from the darkness of this world and seeing the bright moon ahead.

The poem must have been Izumi Shikibu's classic plea for enlightenment when on the verge of death:

Out of the dark   into a road of darkness   I shall enter
Moon of the mountain rim   shine on me from afar

§

On Februrary 21, 1920, in a rowhouse on a narrow side street in the upscale Akasaka district (now part of Minato Ward) of Tokyo, a girl, their first child, was born to Ishigaki Sumi and her husband Hitoshi. The infant's grandfather suggested naming her after his own mother, and so they called her Rin.

Rin grew up in the close-knit society of the traditional urban merchant class, with occasional journeys to the countryside of

---

[1] Notes to the introduction start on page 36.

the Izu Peninsula, her parents' place of origin. Her father Hitoshi, one of the many small businessmen who catered to the high-end restaurants and other establishments of the neighborhood, sold charcoal and firewood, and also owned two sets of wooden rowhouses, a few of which he inhabited or used for business, renting out the rest. His parents lived with them too.

Rin's mother Sumi died in 1924, of injuries suffered in the Great Kantō Earthquake the year before. She left behind a two-month-old baby girl, as well as the four-year-old Rin and a two-year-old boy. Hitoshi's mother cared for the household and children until her own death a mere two years later. The next year, 1927, Rin's father married Kiku, Sumi's younger sister. Kiku feared she would die early like her sister, and she did, in 1929. Rin's father remarried in 1930. This, his third marriage, produced three children, but ended in divorce in 1937. Of the three children, one died at age three and another was adopted by relatives. In 1938, father Hitoshi remarried again, and this time it lasted, although Rin and the fourth wife never got along. In 1942, the girl born just before Sumi's death died herself, only eighteen. Imagine it: by the time she was twenty-two, Rin had lost three beloved mother figures and two siblings and the one mother figure left in her life was a woman she disliked.

She remembered her maternal grandmother in Izu gazing sadly at her and saying, 'Your poverty is not having a mother.'

'Perhaps she was right,' wrote the adult Ishigaki Rin, 'but if so, I was rich in feelings about that poverty.'

Among those feelings was the fear of death. As a child, she sometimes lay in bed at night trembling. During the day, she often imagined live people transformed into corpses. She might be riding in a bus or a tram and see the people ahead of her as they would be in their coffins. She often thought that had she been asked, she would have chosen never to have been born and she wondered why, if there were painless childbirth, there could not also be painless death. The desire to tame such feelings, to turn what was frightening into something outlandishly entertaining, was the soil out of which 'Nursery Rhyme,' with the ghoulish child who thinks people cry over the dead because they taste so bad, later grew:

> When Daddy died they laid
> a white cloth on his face
>
> Just like the white tea towel that's laid
> on the food cooked for dinner
>
> Everyone was crying
> so I realized, Daddy must taste awful,
> awful enough to make them cry

In addition, a number of other poems in this book – 'Traveling On,' 'Flowers,' 'Clams' – take place when the adult poet wakes up alone in the depths of night and has funny, faintly magical encounters with the non-human. Here, too, one feels traces of the childhood fear that made her wakeful at night, but it has grown milder, and the tone is more lyrical.

Ishigaki's father had lived in Tokyo since he was a young man, but he kept the family registration in the southern part of the Izu peninusula (now Matsuzaki in Shizuoka Prefecture). As a young girl, Ishigaki was taken there by either her father or grandfather, but since it was such a long journey, they only rarely went back and then it was, almost without exception, for a family funeral. All her family members who had died were buried there and she herself rests there today. As she later wrote, 'I was born in Tokyo and brought up there, in Akasaka, but if I were a tree, Izu would be my roots.'

Ishigaki Rin was a writer from early childhood and from her mid-teens, she regularly published her free verse poems and fiction in magazines for girls and young women (*shōjo zasshi*) that accepted contributions from their readers. At least in her memory, everyone around her knew she wrote and admired her for it. This was not the case for society at large, where the ideology of 'good wife and wise mother' still held sway. As she explained later, 'When I was a girl, to have a daughter who wrote poetry and loved literature was a calamity (*sainan*) for parents.'

But her father was resigned. He used to say of her 'This one does as she pleases.' She was never sure if it was humblebrag or genuine pique, but she was allowed to do what she wanted. As the eldest, she helped her father when he made his deliveries, but when she went to the neighborhood library and sat for hours reading in the women's section with its few but comfortable easy chairs (the men had to sit at a long table, with seats for more), no one in the family reproached her for not helping out at home.

After graduating from elementary school, the young Ishigaki decided not to go to higher girls' school (*kōtō jogakkō*), as her father hoped and could easily have afforded, but instead to higher elementary school (*kōtō shōgakkō*). To women now, who know the history of their foremothers' struggle for access to higher education, her rejection of higher girls' school – especially since she loved reading and writing so much – may seem puzzling. It helps to know that young Ishigaki, in spite of her intelligence, did not like studying and did not enjoy school. Furthermore, the curriculum of such schools at this time was somewhat like finishing school, designed to make young women into obedient tools of the traditional family system and the nation, rather than strong independent thinkers.

Higher elementary school was only two years, as opposed to the three or even four of girls' school and the courses were of a more commercial bent, but after two years it helped most of its graduates find jobs. This last was its appeal, for 'I felt that if I was not going to obey my family's wishes [to become a dutiful wife and mother] then the least I could do was earn my own keep.' Young Ishigaki also reveled in the thought that she would have her own money to spend on girls' magazines and collections of poetry. When she graduated at the age of fourteen, she immediately went to work in The Industrial Bank of Japan, beginning as an apprentice office worker. When she received her first pay envelope, she was delighted at the freedom it would buy to read and write all she wanted. ('Little did I know,' she later wrote, 'how much of my freedom the money would extract from me.')

Between 1935 and 1943, Ishigaki Rin published over two hundred poems and short stories, the majority in two literary magazines for young women, both dedicated to publishing their subscribers' work. They were *Girls' Garden of Literature* (*Joshi Bun'en*, published 1934–1941) and *Fissure: Women's Poetry* (*Dansō: Jōryūshishi*, published 1938–1943). During this time she was mentored by the poet Fukuda Masao (1893–1952), the poetry editor of *Girls' Garden of Literature* and the guiding spirit behind *Fissure*. Fukuda worked closely with her and the other young women who ran *Fissure*, giving them much advice on writing; but more important than any concrete advice he gave was his belief in their potential as writers in spite of their being women.

Then came war, and the demise of both magazines. During the war, Ishigaki believed wholeheartedly in the divinity of the emperor and the righteousness of Japan's cause, as did most of her personal and literary friends, including Fukuda. She later remembered her attitude with shame:

> When war bulletins came in saying 'It was a great victory!' in my naivete I did not think of the tragedy of the soldiers who had died but only of their bravery. My writing friends were the same. When my younger brother got his draft notice I knelt before him on the tatami and said, 'My deepest congratulations.' That was my mental state.
>
> I went with him to see my aunt in the countryside so that he could say good-bye and she surprised me greatly by telling him, 'Listen, when they say those who are ready to die should step up in front, mind you stay where you are, in

the back.' By the standards of the time, it was an unpatriotic thing to say but her words still ring in my ears.

With its many deprivations and dangers, the war left little room, if any, for literary activity. Ishigaki remained in Tokyo, working at the bank, but 'on May 25, 1945, the Yamanote area of Tokyo was bombed and my whole neighborhood, including our house, burned down.' Both of her younger brothers were away by then, the younger one (like many children during the war) safely evacuated to the countryside, the older one, as we have seen, in the military. The rest of the family (the twenty-five-year-old Ishigaki, her father and step-mother, her paternal grandfather) scattered to various places of refuge. At first, even though all that her father had worked to build up was lost, the destruction of their property and belongings made Ishigaki feel strangely alive, 'as if I had fulfilled a civic duty, and there was a lightness to my step as I rushed about trying to help our neighbors.' But shortly thereafter, as she struggled to make her way to Izu, where her grandfather had taken refuge, the lightheartedness turned to misery, and the readiness to die to a fierce determination to survive.

As it was for all Japanese who lived through the war, the defeat was a major turning point in Ishigaki's life. In a replay of the loss of her house and neighborhood in the fiery air raids a few months earlier, her first emotion was relief and even joy. The first night of peace, when there was no more blackout and 'the lights went on in the fire-devastated streets, the unfamiliar brightness lit a fire in my heart.' This was soon followed by grief, a sense of betrayal, anger, shame, and guilt. Grief at the enormous number of lives lost, and the loss of individual friends and relatives, shock and anger when she realized that everything she had been told about her country and the emperor was a lie.

It was not only anger at the emperor and the country's leaders. She was also disillusioned with herself, ashamed for having been so gullible, and prey to survivor's guilt. And then, as the postwar period went on and Japan regained prosperity, her distrust of government and dislike of certain contemporary trends grew.

This complex of emotions colors such poems as 'An Evening Tale,' 'Living,' 'Cliff,' 'The Rite,' 'Customs,' 'After the Ceremony,' and 'Woman.' There we find a razor-thin border between, on the one side, grief and anger and, on the other, a sense of absurdity that is expressed through wild, surreal images that pop out where you would least expect them. Sometimes it is hard to know whether you should laugh or cry, or both. This balancing act between dark and light is the secret to her art. I think she perfected it when writing the poems about her family in the mid-1950s and early 1960s.

After the war ended in August, the six members of Ishigaki's immediate family slowly regrouped, renting a cramped house of about 350 square feet in a back street of Shinagawa in Tokyo. The family's appalling living conditions and the dependence of them all on daughter Rin to support them by her job at the bank were the inspiration for Ishigaki's searing poems about family in her first two books, including 'Roof,' 'Poverty,' 'House,' 'The Pay Envelope,' 'Rakugo,' 'The Runaway's Song,' and 'Sprouting.' These laments and elaborate curses were levied at the height of pain and yet full of her characteristic humor and daring, surreal imagery. Nothing like them had been seen before.

At the time Ishigaki wrote these poems the family system was already only a shade of its former self, weakened by the new Occupation-imposed constitution and its attendant laws, which included granting women equal rights. Ishigaki retained the sense of duty the family system imposed and, at the same time, her instinctive desire for individual freedom, a contradiction that aroused intense ambivalence. In a sense, she stood between two eras, the traditional and the modern.

Later she came to feel that her sense of obligation was a veil to hide from herself her own dependence on her family. Perhaps, she thought, they all would have been happier had she moved out earlier and stopped being their principal support. She even wondered if writing the family poems had not been 'sinful.' But if it was, she said, 'it was a sin I had to commit in order to survive.' Today, they are considered an important part of her *oeuvre*, for they give voice to the longstanding resentment felt by many, especially women, who sacrificed their own aspirations for the sake of the family, whether the one they were born into or the one into which they married.

Viewed from the perspective of world literature, Ishigaki's poems about the family and the war are among the works that challenge what the pioneering feminist critic Carolyn Heilbrun pointed to as the last taboo for women, the expression of 'anger, together with the open admission of the desire for power and control over one's own life.'

What were the changes in postwar Japan and in her own circumstances that allowed Ishigaki not only to write such poems but to publish them? Answering that means stepping back a bit to look at the general picture.

The immediate postwar years saw a revival of writing and the arts. In spite of paper shortages, rapid inflation, and restrictions imposed by the Occupation authorities, freedom of thought and expression was real. With the abolition of the special police (*tokkō*) and the Peace Preservation Law, and institution of freedom of the press, there was a postwar cultural renaissance, and Ishigaki's poetry played a part. In addition, now that women had been granted equal rights, their opportunities for publication and participation in the literary world increased. There were more women writers than there had been since the Heian period.

Labor union literary magazines were a prominent, though now almost forgotten, feature of the early postwar landscape. The magazines and periodicals that nurtured Ishigaki's early postwar efforts were published in her workplace for her fellow labor union members. In 1951, the first of the yearly anthologies *Poems by Bank Employees* (*Ginkōin no shishū*) was published by the National Federation of Bank Employees' Unions. Well-known writers from the literary world chose the poems from those submitted by union members all over Japan. During the decade that the anthology was published, a number of Ishigaki's works, having already been published in magazines at her workplace, found homes there. Most of the poems in Ishigaki's first collection of poetry, published in 1959, also appeared first in one of the union publications.

Ishigaki narrated these changes from her own individual perspective:

> From my teenage years until I was past twenty my passion for reading and writing was separate from my job. For a woman to write was a kind of shameful thing. One tried to keep it secret from others. I first published my writings in a magazine for young women that solicited its readers' contributions and then in a coterie magazine, both of which ceased publication with the intensification of the war.
>
> I had worked in the bank for eleven years, when in August of 1945, with the defeat, the emperor declared he was human, and the class system and gender discrimination were abolished. After those strange occurrences, Shinto altars were removed from places of business, the formation of labor unions was allowed, and the workplace where I had simply done as I was told changed to a place where you could behave more freely. The conference room was reborn as a place where we all sat around a table with no distinction made between those holding high-ranking positions and those holding low ones, and women could voice their opinions equally with men. We were sorely lacking in foodstuffs and other material things, but union members formed groups for theatre, art, and literature and began to publish their own magazines. We had entered a world that would have been unimaginable before the war.

Now my co-workers asked me to write poetry. I felt a sense of pleasant surprise, and a profound joy, as if the only talent I had could be put to use in building on the ruins. At the same time, the feeling that I was being used evaporated, replaced by the sense that we all shared the workplace. This feeling persisted, at least for a little while.

'Before me the Soup Pot the Rice Pot and the Bright Burning Flame' appeared in a special issue devoted to women, and 'Greetings' was written when they asked me for a poem to accompany the wall newspaper that would have the first picture of the victims of Hiroshima. There were quite a few others too.

'Greetings' was Ishigaki's first poem to gain widespread attention. It was written in August 1952, to mark the anniversary of the atomic bombing of Hiroshima. This is how she recalled its dramatic genesis:

> My writings first attracted notice as creations of someone who worked for a living. After the Second World War, the labor union movement became very active, and as one arm of it, cultural activities flourished. In those days we never had enough of either food or entertainment. Just as we grew our own potatoes and squash in our own small plots, we had to provide our own art, and so we wrote the poems printed in our office newspaper by ourselves. I myself, in fact, was called to the secretariat of the employees' union at my place of work and told: 'Tomorrow is August 6, the day Hiroshima was bombed. In the morning when everyone reports to work and stands in line to stamp their seals in the attendance register, there's going to be a wall newspaper directly over the table, and it will have a photograph of the atomic bomb disaster. We want you to write a poem to go with that photograph right now.' I was given one hour then and there to do it.

I think it was the year that America first allowed publication of photographs of the victims of the atomic bombing. The union executive holding the photograph and telling me to write a poem then and there was himself seeing it for the first time and so was I. We were both profoundly shocked. I responded to his request with the feeling of one crying out in pain when beaten. I have no idea by what method I composed. All I can say is that it was as if that cry turned into something like a drum or a xylophone or both, crashing into each other, and from that shock, words burst forth.

The next morning, the poem was displayed on the wall. I called it 'Greetings,' because it substituted for saying 'Good morning' to my friends. It had been written out in large letters with a brush on a sheet of white paper over three feet high and the width of the entire wall. I entered the office with my co-workers and was taken aback when my own poem 'greeted' me from on high. It was a tremendous surprise that a poem presented in this way would be read by my neighbors.

Ishigaki preferred to compose slowly and thoughtfully, but sometimes the poem came out in a rush, as with 'Greetings.' Another poem like that was 'The Runaway's Song.'

One night in 1961 she was in the throes of composing a poem, probably for one of the cultural festivals sponsored by the labor union, when a line came into her mind unbidden. Things took off from there:

> 'The Runaway's Song' emerged in the small hours of the night. This is unnecessary for my readers to know, but I remember it because the poem arrived suddenly without conscious intent on my part, like one of those monsters of river or forest speaking in my own grumbling voice....
>
> The truth is that I was in the middle of writing another poem, one that had to take fifteen minutes to read aloud,

and I was having a terrible time of it. Suddenly the phrase 'Home – a scab on the face of the earth' floated up from nowhere. Before I could react, a beat began and words rushed in together one after another and presented themselves before me. 'You can't say "an ugly girl," it's not nice,' a voice would say, and I'd think 'Who cares? The poem has to be written!' and I plunged ahead until I reached the last line and with all the words in place came to a standstill. I must have been breathing during that time, but I hardly remember. Of course I made a few changes. And when I made a fair copy later, I added indents after the first line of each stanza. I don't really like this sort of method but in the case of this poem it came together like this naturally….

Now this poem commands me, urges me, like a song coming from outside myself, calling out 'Home – a scab on the face of the earth.' The only thing left for me to do now is to make the move in actuality.

In 1970, five years before retiring from her bank job, and nine years after writing this poem, Ishigaki did leave the house where she had lived with her family since the war's end, and moved to a one-room apartment on her own. Her aloneness was marked in more ways than just parting from the family. It was also society at large that she resisted. In the essay 'Poems with Positions,' she contrasted 'Nameplates,' written in 1966, with the earlier 'Greetings,' written in 1952:

If 'Greetings' is a poem written where I worked, you could say that the next poem was written where I lived. But that's not necessarily why I called it 'Nameplates.' By then, I had pushed union activities a little to one side, and regained a measure of stability. The situation in which I wrote poetry had changed; it was as if I had shifted from being one among many to one within myself.

Explaining further, she added:

> Even if the place you work is almost the inner citadel of capitalism, being intent on the small job before you, you don't notice where you are. Even if the once-strong workers union has become weak, it doesn't show in the expressionless faces of your colleagues who face you as their fingers move over the abacus making sure each and every yen is accounted for. However, when election season begins, matters change as sound trucks appear in the station plaza, and eventually certain things gravitate to the area where I sit.
>
> We used to openly declare our support for a political party and debate things in the workplace newspaper but in 1966 such controversies did not arise. The atmosphere was such that you would politely avoid bringing up political matters. At the same time secret invitations from those who opposed the ruling party would come to the desks of even insignificant people like me.
>
> When it comes to poetry and my way of living I lean to the conservative, but adding a single vote to the current conservative political entities is one thing I won't do. I begin from that position and walk my own way. Then a truck approaches and invites me to get in, offering me a ride. I vacillate, unsure whether I can trust that person's driving. When I get home, religious solicitations come. They say 'the only way for you to attain happiness is to enter our organization, and if you don't your family will have more and more ill fortune and misery.' It's a nauseating kind of kindness, closer to coercion, and makes me horribly angry, but when it's someone who lives nearby or a neighbor, it's hard to know how to deal with it.
>
> 'Nameplates' is a simple poem about nameplates but at the time little things like the above that were in the back of my mind happened to fuse with unrelated memories about nameplates and became a poem.

I wrote it pretty quickly but until almost the last minute I went back and forth about whether or not to make 'and as for' or 'on' precede 'the home of your soul.' Geographically speaking, I was going back and forth around the vicinity of Ochanomizu Station, walking with 'and as for' and 'on.' Finally I realized that 'and as for' was the only possible choice. I felt that 'on' would be more precise but at the same time it would narrow the poem.

Ishigaki lived alone from 1970 until her death thirty-four years later. In 1987 she summed up her relationship to poetry and to words:

All I've done is live, work, and write a little. That's it.
Maybe that's why when I don't work I feel like I don't have anything to write about. And in my case it seems to be my hands and my legs, more than my head, that think.
I'd like to ask them if I'm right about them, but they are mute.
At any rate, poetry is my internal rhythm, the outlines of my thought, my way of structuring life, the shape of prayer, another language I've made in my own way. I've brought forth this imperfect way of communicating with all my heart, as frustrated as a child just learning to speak trying to express things it can barely get its tongue around.
I'm not seeking poetry, and I don't write for the sake of poetry, so even if I don't write anything tomorrow or am reborn in a completely different form, I don't think I'd mind.
The home was bondage, the workplace subservience. Everyday life was one thing after another to put up with. There was only one thing I did because I wanted to do it, a space where I could do as I pleased, and that was poetry. Of course it was selfish of me. If even poetry had found a way to bind me, I doubt that I would have stayed with it.
But I've lived among words for many years and these days

what amazes me is how wonderful they are. I can't express it well but I feel they are a kind of wealth. Words have the power to bring people infinite riches. Fortunately, they do not obey the rules of private property, so this power is accessible to everyone. No one has to pay for the right to use the personal pronoun 'I.' That, I think, is an excellent thing.

During her lifetime, Ishigaki published the four volumes of poetry and the several uncollected poems that were my sources for the translations in this book, as well as the essays and anthologies mentioned above. At least two publishers wanted to publish another volume of her poems during her lifetime, but their plans did not come to fruition. Meanwhile, she had good friends (including the poet Ibaragi Noriko) whom she met for meals and with whom she traveled around Japan, and she gave several interviews (including a three-hour one to me in 1998, over coffee at the Tokyo Station Hotel, one of her favorite haunts), but she never invited anyone to her small apartment. A legend arose among her friends, which may have been begun by Ishigaki herself, that aspiring poets sent her so many books and coterie magazines that for lack of space she had to spread her futon bedding on top of them or else put them on the apartment's veranda in order to sleep.

By December 26, 2004, when she died after a few years of increasing ill health and frailty, Ishigaki's poetry and essay collections had all been reprinted, some several times and sometimes with the addition of as yet uncollected poems. She had also received several important literary prizes, and was considered a major contemporary poet.

By then her younger brother was the only family member left. He was cared for in an institution that had an attached hospital and it was in that hospital that Ishigaki spent the last few weeks of her life, so they were able to live close together again. I have always been moved by the photograph taken of them at that time – both are smiling, their heads close together.

Three hundred people turned out for the memorial service held at the Yamanoue Hotel in Tokyo on February 7, 2005, and when it was over Ishigaki's brother stood up from his seat in the front row, turned around, and with a gentle smile thanked us all, on behalf of his sister, for coming.

Ishigaki Rin with her brother Ishigaki Toshiharu,
a few weeks before her death in 2004.
Courtesy of Minamiizu-chō Public Library.

§

The difference between war and peace, the Japanese past and present, was one of Ishigaki's great themes. Nevertheless, the tenor of her poetry tends towards the future, often a dystopian one. In 'Greetings,' written in memory of the bombing of Hiroshima, only the first few lines are about that past event; the rest is about future undefinable disasters that she begs her audience to be ready for. In the uncollected 'Mistake' (*Ayamachi*, 1970), part of a long series of poems on the severely polluted city of Yokkaichi, her statement is even clearer:

> Sleep in peace
> Because we will not repeat the mistake
>
> Those were the words on the cenotaph, of Hiroshima.
>
> When it comes to   mistakes
> we are always wrong
> we obsess about a past mistake
> and always make
> a new one

In 'The Twilight Crane,' she watches as the earth forsakes human beings:

> The earth
> is drifting away from human beings
> It's getting
> smaller and
> small
> er

This quietly apocalyptic poem, first published in 1970, must be one of the earliest eco-poems in Japanese literature.

At the same time, the poet's eyes were also fixed firmly on the present. Ishigaki is a kind of cartographer, mapping the spaces and the activities of her world: the public bath, the home, toilets, kitchens, the workplace, food shopping, cooking, her own bedroom, funerals, and so on. Her postwar poetry was often called 'life poetry' or 'poetry of daily life' (*seikatsushi*) for this reason, and stress is laid on its social and political dimensions.

Those quotidian spaces often enlarge or dissolve into other dimensions, places of dream, fantasy, and imagination. The events that then occur happen in the same quotidian spaces but they are invisible to the eye. The realistic kitchen of 'Before Me the Soup Pot the Rice Pot and the Bright Burning Flame' is a warm and comfortable one, with women standing before the pots and pans; but the kitchen of 'Living' is more like the lair of a wild beast, a surreal place littered not only with carrot tops and fishbones, but also with 'Daddy's guts.' By the end of the poem it feels less like a kitchen than the ruins of her own life.

The boundary between death and life is especially porous, much as it was for Ishigaki in childhood, when she fantasized about living people lying dead in their coffins. In 'The Book of the Dead,' death becomes part of a game of hide and seek. In 'Yesterday's Faces,' playmates of old and the ghosts of those playmates are indistinguishable. In 'Tree,' she converses about death with a tree that stands at the entrance to a cemetery. In 'Customs,' the dead come back to wander among the living. In 'After the Ceremony,' the boundary between life and death collapses when the dead soldiers appear to claim their medals.

Ishigaki lived, then, not only in the quotidian world but in another, interior and invisible one. Here she was acutely aware of the seamless and endless flow of time and of the arbitrariness of the divisions humanity makes in it. As the year approached its end, she wrote:

> Opening the window, I can't keep from saying to the clouds 'It's the end of the year!' but they don't answer. Why should they? They have nothing to do with the divisions human beings blithely make in the smooth unbroken flow of eternity.

The habit of speaking to (and sometimes with) everything alive, animal, vegetable or mineral, clouds, trees, clams, is essential to Ishigaki's identity as a poet. In her early teens, while sketching on the roof of her school, she had even fantasized marrying the sky and was certain that she would give birth to a cloud. In her poetry, such conversations, one-sided or not, happen most often when she wakes at night, or when she is alone. In this parallel life she is in communion with time itself, personified as the spirit of autumn ('Traveling On'), or lingering nearby as the flowers in her room move towards death ('Flowers'). There is a kind of poignancy to the events in this invisible world:

> When I have trouble falling asleep or when I wake up in the middle of the night, I feel forlorn in the dark and there is also a kind of regret, as though time itself were flowing through the dark. (*Honō* 28)

In many of Ishigaki's poems, the 'I' is ungendered in a way that feels intentional, as if to allow her greater freedom of expression ('Rakugo' and 'Nameplates,' for example), but in other poems, she speaks in an unambiguous female voice. These include 'These Days I,' 'Secret,' 'This Overflowing Light,' 'The Shoes that Slipped Off,' and 'Seascape.' If one were to imagine an actual human being in them, it would be (except for 'This Overflowing Light') a woman in early middle age, keenly aware of her reproductive life coming to an end, who has sought love, briefly found it, considered marriage and motherhood and rejected both, and then resolved to go on alone, rejecting the intimacy of a sexual relationship. In fact, during the interview mentioned earlier, when I shyly asked her if 'The Shoes that Slipped Off' had anything to do with a relationship, she replied without hesitation that it was about a failed love affair, *shitsuren*. But the backstory is not important. What matters is the mental space she arrives at after that difficult journey.

In 'Seascape,' the 'I' of the poem is alienated from ordinary people and their ordinary lives on land; the poem begins with her declaration 'I'm a pure red ocean.' She was right when she wrote that often she spoke like a child just learning to speak. The poem's central words are delphic; they might be uttered by a sibyl or a shaman, or even be a magic riddle:

> What I chewed up at table was rocks
> what I spoke to in town was sand
> what I embraced in the forest was the wind

I take the lines to mean, in everyday words, that even when the 'I' of this poem tried to believe that she was an ordinary person and ate, talked, and loved among ordinary people, she was actually still an ineradicable part of nature, like the ocean, and interacting with stone, sand, and wind, elements that, just like she herself, drift about the shore, the boundary between sea and land. The mind that utters these lines transcends the human. From this standpoint, her conversations with trees and clouds in other contexts make perfect sense.

Looking back on Ishigaki's life, I see that the terrible times of the war and the early postwar period, traumatic as they were, were valuable to a poet who could survive them. The photograph of Hiroshima might have left another person speechless with pity and shock. Instead, Ishigaki's emotions demanded expression in words. The suffering and tribulations of her family life might have exhausted someone else, but instead inspired some of her best work. Somewhere, even when at her most despairing (I think here of the grotesquely funny image of the spineless octopus in 'Sprouting' who has retreated to total passivity), she found the strength and the desire to write.

What were the roots of this impulse? Such things can never be wholly known, but surely one factor was that writing itself was a habit for her, one she had practiced from childhood. Also, in contrast to her prewar activities, when the literary mainstream was dominated by men and her publications were restricted to women's magazines, there was now a new audience consisting of her fellow union members, plus the cultural renaissance described above. Her poetry, insofar as it helped people make sense of the trauma of the war and the chaos of the new world, became necessary not just to herself but to others as well. With the rise of second-wave feminism in the 1960s and 1970s, her poetry became even more meaningful.

Perhaps most important, however, was her attachment to words, and her almost physical sense of their power. Related to that, was her sense of a dimension of existence that words could invoke, a dimension immune to human intervention – call it nature, eternity, what you will – and one to which she felt an unbreakable connection. This instinctive awareness of a larger dimension had, I believe, been with her from early on: it was what she called 'this overflowing light' in that eponymous poem. In an essay, she explained that the poem was a dialogue between her younger self and her older self. The younger one loved 'this overflowing light of spring,' and did not want to leave it, but at the same time wondered if she should become a mother.

Not only was the light there in the spring of her life, but she remained connected to it as she went on through the darkness, another reality as strong and vital as that of the everyday.

There is a tendency to think of Ishigaki as a dark poet, with a streak of surreal humor, and also a poet of resistance, and so she is. But along with an innate self-confidence that gave her the courage to reject the ordinary path for women, from early on her inner world connected her to eternity and the vastness of the universe. The light of this other dimension illuminates many of her strongest poems.

Notes

15 'Do you think I can get along': Ishigaki Rin, 'Shikenkan ni irete,' *Yūmoa no Sakoku,* Chikuma Bunko Series i–7–1, Chikuma Shobō, 1987, 73. (Hereafter *Yūmoa no sakoku* is abbreviated to *Sakoku.*)

15 'Out of the dark': *Kuraki yori / kuraki michi ni zo / irinubeki / Haruka ni terase / yama no ha no tsuki.* From the imperial poetry anthology *Shūi Wakashū* (c. 1005) xx:1342.

15 On February 21, 1920: This and other dates are either from Ishigaki's own essays or from 'Ishigaki Rin Jihitsu Nenpu,' *Ishigaki Rin Shishū* (Iwanami Bunko 200–1, Iwanami Shoten, 2016), ed. Ito Hiromi, 315–325.

15 The infant's grandfather suggested naming her: Ishigaki Rin, 'Watashi no namae,' *Yoru no taiko,* Chikuma Bunko Series i–7–3, Chikuma Shobō, 2001, 187. (Hereafter *Yoru no taiko* is abbreviated to *Taiko.*)

16 Izu, her parents' place of origin: 'Natsu no higure ni,' *Sakoku,* 59.

16 Her father Hitoshi, one of the many small businessmen: Ishigaki Rin, 'Tsukiai no me,' *Honō ni te wo kazashite*, Chikuma Bunko Series i–7–2, Chikuma Shobō, 1992, 161–162; 'Hosohimo,' ibid, 164; 'Rainen irrashai,' ibid, 245. (Hereafter *Honō ni te wo kazashite* is abbreviated to *Honō.*)

16 Rin and the fourth wife never got along: 'Katachi,' *Honō,* 198.

16 She remembered her maternal grandmother: 'Shi wo kaku koto to, ikiru koto,' *Sakoku,* 163–164.

16 Among those feelings was the fear: 'Dekiru koto dekinai koto,' *Sakoku,* 246.

17 Ishigaki's father [...] kept the family registration: 'Shunshū,' *Honō,* 143; 'Katachi,' *Honō,* 195; 'Izu to watashi,' *Taiko,* 199.

17 'I was born in Tokyo': 'Hana yo sora wo tsuke,' *Sakoku,* 112.

17 Ishigaki Rin was a writer from early childhood: 'Shi wo kaku koto to, ikiru koto,' *Sakoku,* 163; 'Kiru hito, tsukuru hito,' *Honō,* 43; 'Tsuzurikata,' *Honō,* 95–96.

18 At least in her memory, everyone around her: 'Inaka no anderusen,' *Honō*, 126; 'Izu to watashi,' *Taiko*, 201.
18 'When I was a girl': 'Tachiba no aru shi,' *Sakoku*, 200.
18 'This one does as she pleases': 'Shikenkan ni irete,' *Sakoku*, 70.
18 As the eldest, she helped her father: 'Hi ni naru toki,' *Honō*, 231–232.
19 When she graduated at the age of fourteen: 'Okazaki Shukurō sensei,' *Honō*, 152–153.
19 'Little did I know': 'Shi wo kaku koto to, ikiru koto,' *Sakoku*, 164.
19 Between 1935 and 1943: Hata Natsuki, 'Ishigaki Rin no shoki sakuhin: *Dansō Joshi Bun'en Shōjo Gahō* keisai sakuhin wo megutte' (Ishigaki Rin's Early Works: On works in *Dansō, Joshi Bun'en*, and *Shōjo Gahō*), *Jissen Kokubungaku*, 88:5, 2015, 110–112. http://id.nii.ac.jp/1157/00001388/; and Takenaka Noriko and Nishihara Daisuke, 'Ishigaki Rin Senzen Happyō Sakuhin Ichiran' (List of Ishigaki Rin's Works 1935–1943), *Hiroshima Daigaku Nihongo Kyōiku Kenkyū*, No. 28, 2013, 13–20. http://doi.org/10.15027/45443
19 'When war bulletins came in': 'Shi wo kaku koto to, ikiru koto,' *Sakoku*, 170–171.
20 'On May 25 [...] our house': 'Shi wo kaku koto to, ikiru koto,' *Sakoku*, 171. This was the Great Yamanote Air Raid, one of the worst wartime firebombings of urban Tokyo areas. It reduced most of the Akasaka and Aoyama districts to ashes, 3,242 people died, 559,683 became homeless, and 16.8 square miles of Tokyo were incinerated. (Richard Sams, 'Inferno on the Omotesando: The Great Yamanote Air Raid,' *Asia-Pacific Journal Japan Focus*, May 25, 2015, Volume 13, Issue 21, Number 1. https://apjjf.org/-Richard-Sams/4321/article.pdf)
20 'as if I had fulfilled': 'Yūmoa no sakoku,' *Sakoku*, 81.
20 But shortly thereafter, as she struggled: 'Katachi,' *Honō*, 193–194.

20 'The lights went on': 'Kurashi no shūhen,' *Honō*, 29.
21 Later she came to feel: Ishigaki Rin, *Shi no okurimono 3 Katei no shi*, Chikuma Shobō, 1981, 19–22. Also 'Harigami,' *Taiko*, 62.
22 'it was a sin I had to commit': Ishigaki Rin, *Shi no okurimono 3 Katei no shi*, Chikuma Shobō, 1981, 22.
22 'anger, together with the open admission': Carolyn Heilbrun, *Writing a Woman's Life*, New York: Ballantine Books, 1989, 13.
22 There were more women writers: Donald Keene, *Dawn to the West: Japanese Literature in the Modern Era: Fiction*, New York: Holt, Rinehart, and Winston, 1984, 1162.
23 'From my teenage years': 'Jisaku ni tsuite,' *Taiko*, 169, 173–174; 'Hana yo, sora wo tsuke,' *Sakoku*, 110.
24 'My writings first attracted notice': 'Tachiba no aru shi,' *Sakoku*, 185–186, 188–189.
25 '"The Runaway's Song" emerged in the small hours': 'Tachiba no aru shi,' *Sakoku*, 195, 198–199.
26 'If "Greetings" is a poem': 'Tachiba no aru shi,' *Sakoku*, 190.
27 'Even if the place you work': 'Tachiba no aru shi,' *Sakoku*, 192–193.
27 'the inner citadel of capitalism': At that time, The Industrial Bank of Japan, where Ishigaki worked, was one of the largest banks in the world and had ties with many powerful corporations. (In 2002, it merged with Dai-ichi Kangyo Bank and Fuji Bank to form the Mizuho Financial Group.)
27 'those who opposed the ruling party': that is, Communists, whose party had been crushed, making political debate risky.
28 'I wrote it pretty quickly': Ishigaki was vacillating between *seishin no aribasho mo* and *seishin no aribasho ni*. 'And as for' is my translation of *mo*, which literally means 'and,' 'also,' or 'as well.' 'On' is a literal translation of the particle *ni*. In Japanese these particles come after the noun phrase, not before it.
28 'All I've done is live': 'Shi wo kaku koto to, ikiru koto,' *Sakoku*, 177–178.

29 At least two publishers: Dōwaya, owned by Tanaka Kazuo, and Kashinsha, owned by Ōkubo Kenichi. Tanaka compiled *Remon to Nezumi* (Dōwaya, 2008), a small posthumous collection, from manuscripts of uncollected poems found in Ishigaki's apartment after her death (*Remon to Nezumi*, 155).

29 A legend arose: Kakehashi Kumiko, 'Kono chichi arite shijin Ishigaki Rin (6),' *Nihon Keizai Shimbun*, June 26, 2021.

29 some several times: For example, *Gendaishi Bunko 46 Ishigaki Rin Shishū*, one of several volumes of Ishigaki's selected works put out by various publishers, was first published by Shichōsha in 1971, has been reprinted twenty-three times since then, and as of 2022 was still in print. Since its first printing, eighty thousand copies have been sold. (Information provided by Shichōsha's Itsuki Takebayashi, August, 2022).

31 her statement is even clearer: Ishigaki wrote 'Mistake' in 1970 as part of a suite of poems for a television documentary about the polluted city of Yokkaichi. The original text is in *Gendaishi Bunko 46 Ishigaki Rin Shishū*, Shichōsha, 1994, 107; the full poem is not translated here.

32 'Opening the window': 'Toshi no kure,' *Honō*, 59.

33 in her early teens, while sketching: 'When I was in upper elementary school, I would go up to the roof after school and draw pictures of the clouds and so on in my sketchbook, thinking "I'll marry the sky and for sure I'll give birth to a cloud."' 'Watashi wa naze kekkon shinai ka,' *Honō*, 214.

33 'When I have trouble falling asleep': 'Machi ni akari ga tsuita hi,' *Honō*, 28.

34 I take these lines to mean: My thanks to Yasuhiro Yotsumoto for help with these difficult lines.

35 In an essay she explained: 'Shi wo kaku koto, ikiru koto,' *Sakoku*, 175. Ishigaki also discusses the poem in 'Uta,' *Sakoku*, 11–12.

The Industrial Bank of Japan in the 1950s.

from

Before Me

the Soup Pot the Rice Pot

and the Bright Burning Flame (1959)

私の前にある鍋とお釜と燃える火と

Greetings

On a photograph of the atomic bombing

Oh, this face
so horribly burned
one of the hideous burns of the 250,000
people who were in Hiroshima
on August 6 1945

is no longer in this world

and yet
dear friend
look again at our faces
as we turn to each other
today's healthy faces
morning's fresh and open faces
that show no trace of the fires of war

I search those faces for tomorrow's expression
and I shudder

the earth holds hundreds of atomic bombs
and you are walking the hair's-breadth border between
    life and death
how can you be so tranquil
and so beautiful

hush listen closely
don't you hear something approaching
what we must see plainly is in front of our eyes
what we must choose
rests in our hands

eight-fifteen in the morning
returns each day

all the 250,000 people who died
in one instant on the morning of August 6 1945
like you   like me
who are here now
were tranquil   were beautiful   were unprepared

(*August* 1952)

An Evening Tale

When Kuboyama the fisherman
died of Bikini's ashes
the newspaper headlines screamed
CONSOLATION MONEY 5.5 MILLION YEN,
a pitiful spectacle it was,
the reporters of a penniless country splashing the story
on their front pages for their penniless public

But who am I to talk
an outrageous and equally pitiful thought occurs to me
if I could leave that much money to my family
wouldn't my death give them more joy than my life?

The money itself
might even attend the funeral in the shape of bills
larger than life, strutting around like
Gulliver among the Lilliputians

The 80-year-old woman next door used to get angry
when her family prayed at the household altar
are you trying to pray me dead? she'd say
until, that is, only ten years late, thirty-five thousand yen
      consolation money
for the son she'd lost in the war arrived, bringing her joy
this will pay my funeral expenses, she crowed

A short-lived joy, that was –
in less than a month she was dead

But the terrible thing is
the family took the money and spent it on themselves
so they can't hold the funeral –
the whole neighborhood is abuzz with it

His story and hers
couldn't be less alike, yet
somewhere there's a thread between

(*September* 1954)

In a Hundred Human Bellies

On the table a hundred plates
before the plates a hundred people
on the plates a hundred flounders,

amid the sound of dishes scraping faintly against each other
the fish shrink down to bone, head, tail
(if the Princess of the Oceans saw this, she'd throw a fit!)
A hundred ladies & gentlemen
wipe their lips on spotless napkins, pronounce in elegant tones
'Dear me, what's the world coming to these days?'

In a hundred human bellies
a hundred piscine stiffs

Before Me the Soup Pot the Rice Pot
and the Bright Burning Flame

For a long time
it was always these they placed before us
women,

soup pots we could handle with ease and
rice pots just right for making plump
moist grains of lustrous rice and the glowing flame
that was ours from earliest times
these were always before our mothers, and
grandmothers, and their mothers too

What quantities
of love and faith those people
must have poured into these vessels,
sometimes in the shape of red carrots
at other times black kelp
or again fish minced up fine

In the kitchen they always prepared
the meals on time
morning noon and evening
and always several sat waiting, laps warm, hands too

Ah were it not for those who sat waiting
how could the women have kept on
cheerfully making meals again and again?
They were portraits of limitless affection
of daily unconscious devotion

Why cooking was apportioned to women
as their duty is a riddle
but I can not think it a calamity,
even if it has kept us back in knowledge, and in status
it's not too late
while before us remain
the soup pot and the rice pot, and the bright burning flame

with feeling as deep
as when with these cherished vessels
we cook meat and potatoes,
let's study politics and economics and literature,

not for the sake of pride or glory but
all and always
to provide sustenance for human beings
all and always our efforts infused with love

The Women's Bath

On midnight of December 31 1957
piping hot clouds of steam blanket the public bath
the crowd bobbing and bumping like potatoes
    washed in a barrel

The bathwater
muddied with skin oils and grime
adrift with seaweedy wisps of twisted hair and what not
fairly bubbles, overflowing
with the humans in it and their abundant blood,

while on the flooded shores
the soap – 25 yen a bar at most – brews a sudsy foam
and of that whiteness, to the New Year turned, is Venus born

This is a gossamer legend of Tokyo grown from the lives of
the ordinary people who dwell in its alleys and byways

A chill wind blows as the door slides open
and a pepper-and-salt perm   washed hair seal-slick,
one hand held modestly in front of her,
steps out into the world from a shell of which
one half is past, the other future

the shabby clothes awaiting her in a bamboo basket
all she knows of her own true 'rights'

And this is how the Venus of Japan
comes to be in a painting even older than
Botticelli's,

in a culture and civilization
that still give off the stench of ammonia
a primeval swamp
of a bathtub

There Is In This World

There is in this world, one and one knot only
made of that light
beyond that far horizon
one and one knot only
to untie it
I was born
I am rushing towards the horizon
who could know?
I'm sure I'll succeed in a flash
– just like a soaring star –
unnoticed by a million people
'Good-bye, humans'
I fly off from there a butterfly
into weightless clouds, then endless overflowing springs
gentle breezes
ah from there ocean, mountains, sky
infinitely unfolding
and then again that horizon
I go, I go, I go and yet –

The Watcher

The flowers have scattered,
just like shooting stars
'How many thousands of years till their light reaches earth?'
Flowers, it will be many thousands of years from now
that they fall into   the deep earth
you fall, flowers
last year, this year, next year too

your one and only life falls and falls,
and who sees?
Who is the watcher…

0

Zero is 0
0 is round
the roundness of the universe, the horizon, an apple

an apple with its red skin, whiteness within
bite and it makes a crisp-crunch sound
the tangy sweetness of that full ripe 0

And then there's the roundness
of soap bubbles, their intangible softness
their rainbow shine   floating up in the air they look
light to the casual eye, but the weight within makes
      them   burst
wonderously they appear in our world only to disappear
ephemeral 0's

tree leaves rustle, moving in circles
a stone thrown in a pond makes a circle of ripples

0
zero
the basis of 1
full and complete are the zeros of this world!
People live inside 0
people fade to zero in the end,

nothing can support the weight of the universe
and yet it appears in the heavens so lightly
only to disappear   ephemeral 0
so many centuries within that 0, the others, the others,
      and me!

*

I'll blow up 0,
like a rubber balloon, with my own warm breath
all the 0's in the world
I'll huff and I'll puff and hold on tight
until I make infinite emptiness round and full

I'll swell the clear blue sky
the cold horizon
with all the life in me,

how do you like it?
The earth is light
so is the universe

the rubber balloon blown up with my breath, floats up high
into the center of the magnificent heavens
sparkling, shining

The Sea and Apples

A steamship is passing along the coast of western Izu

from a bus on the cliffs looking down
you'd see what seems   a green field on a quiet day
but is really the sea
a glittering green surface
and slowly, a small boat moving across it

I was in that boat,
the deck was plenty big enough for me
the sea was brimful to the boat's gunwale
the sea was brimful to the shore too
in the palm of my hand I happily held
a red apple
larger than my palm and just the right weight

October, an autumn overflowing with ripe apples
and a boat supported by the tides
and me supported by the boat

Oh sea
I felt your weight in the palm of my hand,
in the distance Fuji was standing
cloudless
I was standing on the deck
everything swayed

a steamship is passing by the coast of western Izu,

from a village path you'd see it disappear behind a tiny island
it's small, that boat

Roof

Japanese houses have low roofs
the poorer the family the lower the roof,

the lowness of the roof

weighs me down

Where does the heaviness come from
I step back a little to take a good look
what's above the house
is not the blue of the sky but
something the deep dark color of blood

Something that clutches me and bars the way
something that traps me in this cramped dwelling
and sucks up my strength,

my invalid father lives up on the roof
so do my stepmother
and my brothers too

On top of that flimsy
corrugated tin roof
of barely 10 *tsubo*
that flaps and rattles
in a puff of wind,
I see a fat white daikon
and some rice
and a nice warm bed

Carry me says this roof
and under its weight
I, a woman, feel my spring darken
in the distance the sun goes down

Poverty

When I start grumbling
my father says
'Try to be patient, I'll be out of the way soon'
as if he was a piece of old furniture

That's no comfort
that's a threat I say
losing my temper, but

when my grandfather died last year
he left behind one tatami mat of extra space,
which in this cramped house was a huge help

I wept as I walked in the funeral procession but
the near and distant relatives
all murmured consolingly
'That's a load off your shoulders now,'
and that was the farewell,
to the grandfather who loved me best of all

A year later my father
now half-paralyzed in the same way
soothes me from the bed he
shares with my invalid step-mother saying
it won't be long now just try to put up with it,

a day will come when these terrible memories
will replace my living father
and from these recollections there will be
no exit

The Pay Envelope

Once a month on pay day, I receive a tan envelope
20 centimeters high
by 14 wide

Its thickness signals one month's labor, weighed on a scale
the bills and coins like a counterweight that
brings my life barely into balance,

what a convenient envelope it is
from the moment it's in my hands I'm opening and closing it
Like this world of mine where day and night alternate
sometimes when I extract a wrinkled old bill
today's sky softly opens blue above my head

Stores on the shopping street all lined up
goods half out on the street
in piles so high they may spill over
but all that stuff is money in a transparent safe,
fresh-laid eggs
red apples
even the heaped sardines looking like they've just been
    scooped from the sea
something is standing guard over them,
to fend off even the innocently extended hands of children
the constant sound of footsteps like a watchman
patrolling the hallways of a bank

That's when I take out another bill from my pay envelope,
fit its face amount to the keyhole and with sure skill
open up that transparent safe,
along the way even making
the mouth holes of the vendors open bright with smiles

At rush hour on the train I'm elbowed and shoved so
day by day this envelope gets grubbier and
as weary as its owner
When the very last coin is gone
it's time to toss it but just in case, I peek inside,
and ooh look who's here, look who's here

The inside is lined with twelve ragged tatami mats
and from the mouth of the envelope
my old parents and my younger brothers are saying
all right then, off you go to work again tomorrow

How can I throw it away
this little envelope with its corrugated tin roof
that a gust of wind would blow away
carrot tops and fish bones spilling out from the kitchen

The pay envelope isn't a bag of tricks or a sorcerer's pouch
but then where did the months and days I poured into it go
when I look for them
the bills have melted into air
and only an empty envelope is left in my hand

Getting Ready

Is that decay

that eager moment when a hundred thousand trees
as one shrug off their every leaf from top to toe

the sun pours down its clear gaze so intently
that their bodies almost burn
the wind clings to their branches crying peel off those clothes

then apple branches sag beneath their own weight
and the juice of the grapes grows heavy, sweetness
dribbling from rounded fruits

autumn
this opulent autumn
what is there to regret, what to mourn
all I have I fling away
stretch my hands to the sky
this is all my will, all my desire!

With each day the sky grows clearer, brighter, deeper
I become a tree arrowing through its very depths

is that decay,
that eager moment when as one the trees
shrug off their every leaf from top to toe –

never have I known my life as I do now
deep within my body, I embrace a distant spring
and my face turns quietly towards winter, ready, waiting

These Days I

Would you call it the ocean's last full tide
The fullness and weight of my breasts in my hands!

The apples are ready to pick
the best fish now is the autumn saury
fat shining, in its succulent prime
(suddenly awake, startled at the warm flesh, my very own)

this is the peak of the life given
to living things that perish in the end

as the wind rustles in the trees
as the dew shines on the blossoms
so in the end they will wither, they will scatter
for all that lives there is but one season

under this beautiful shining sun
how will the blossoms scatter
how will the trees bear their fruit
with uneasy heart these days, I
think about preparations for the end

Secret

I'll birth a bird   and teach it how to sing
I'll raise a butterfly   and teach it how to dance
diving into water I'll birth a fish
ascending to light I'll nurture the wind
if I dress them all in human clothes I've sewn
what will people call them
      the cow birthed a calf
      and dressed it all in cow clothes
      the horse birthed a foal
      and dressed it all in horse clothes
I'll mingle warmly with the mothers of all living things
and bring up my children lightly in the shadows of the world

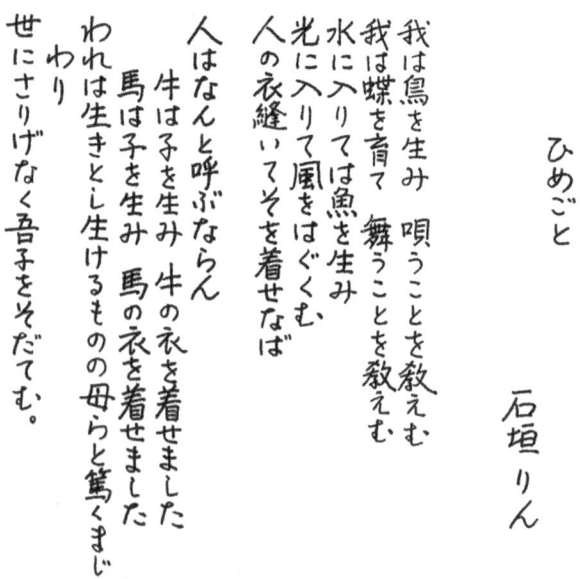

Manuscript of 'Secret' in Ishigaki Rin's own hand.
Courtesy of Minamiizu-chō Public Library.

This Overflowing Light

Mother, can't I stay here   forever like this?
The flowers so beautiful, the sky so blue, why must they
pass away, from this overflowing light   of spring –

    *

Young lady   young lady
the clouds are flowing by
where are they flowing to
so far so far away
tell me my pretty one
where you will go

    *

I'm not even sure what
the strange thing called a human being   really is
will it do to follow the way of everything alive
and become   a mother, I ask my heart
but how can it answer
each day each night   like a lullaby I hum   to myself
  the squirrel births a squirrel
  the snake births a snake
fine then   should I become a mother
not easy to answer   the heart has no reply –

The Shoes That Fell Off

Outside me was filled with air
inside me was filled with something similar
or maybe lighter

I painted my face
filling in the eyebrows and applying lipstick
then softly let myself stand up, for all to see

My shoes anchored me to earth like weights,
kept me from
floating upward

I laughed
I was cross
I talked
I worked and got my pay

One day, because someone embraced
this human being made of a rubber balloon
my shoes fell off

The balloon floated up,
away from houses
from shopping streets
from people

   (Where did we come apart?)

The farther I go the more alone I am
in the middle of the sky
the balloon is rising

from

Nameplates and More (1968)

表札など

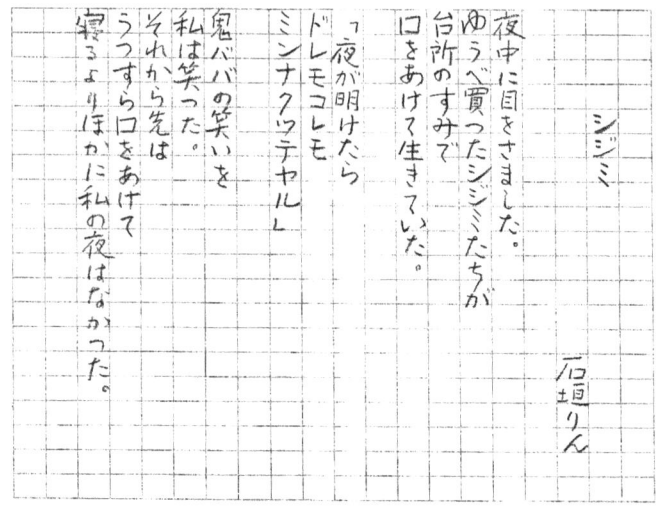

Manuscript of 'Little Clams' in Ishigaki Rin's own hand.
Courtesy of Minamiizu-chō Public Library.

Little Clams

Woke up in the dead of night
In a corner of the kitchen
the little clams I'd bought that evening
were alive mouths open

'Come dawn
I'll gobble you up
each and every one'

Let out a cackle
like an evil old witch
After that couldn't help it had to
sleep all night with mouth ajar

Nameplates

Wherever you live nothing beats putting
the nameplate up by yourself

It never bodes well when someone else
affixes the nameplate to the space
where you spend your nights

In the hospital
they added Miss to
the name on the sickroom door
Miss Ishigaki Rin it said

Stay at an inn
and the room's unnamed
but in the end they'll put me
inside a cremation oven and
dangle a tag from the door that says
the Honorable Ishigaki Rin,
how'll I object then?

Miss
the Honorable
a hex on them both,

wherever you live nothing comes close
to attaching the nameplate with your own two hands

And as for the home of your soul
never let anyone else hang up the nameplate but you
Ishigaki Rin
will do thank you

Living

You can't live without eating
Rice
vegetables
meat
air
light
water
parents
siblings
teachers
money and hearts too
Without eating them I could never have lived
I pat my full stomach
wipe my lips
the kitchen is littered
with carrot tops
chicken bones
Daddy's guts
the fading light of forty
For the first time my eyes weep a wild beast's tears

Traveling On

Suddenly I was awake and
autumn was by my bed

I've come a long way, it says
so I ask, from last year
from more before, it replies

The year before last, I ask
and it says, much farther back than that

So I ask
then the autumn that came to my place last year what was that
That was a different autumn,
it says
last year's autumn that was – by now it's gone on way ahead

When you say way ahead do you mean the future, I ask
And am told
no not at all,
the future means something coming later, right?
I'm stumped for a reply

So I ask, then has it gone towards the past

It can't go back to the past, it says,
in that way it's like you

Autumn
was by my bed
I've come from far away, it says
Let's go on far ahead, it says

Flowers

wake up suddenly late at night ...

    huge chrysanthemums stirring
    in a corner of my room
    tomorrow signs of decay will appear
    on this beauty of their full bloom and
    they'll have to leave the beauty behind and set off
    on a long journey and with that ahead there's no way
    those flowers can sleep because they're
    all getting ready

... at the hush of that crush

Island

I'm standing in a tall mirror
A lonely
little island
Apart from everyone

I know
the island's history
Its measurements
Bust waist and hips
What it wears in every season
Its chirping birds
Its hidden spring
The fragrance of its flowers

I live
on my island
Clearing the land, building on it
And yet
I can't know everything
about this island
Nor can I live here forever

I look in the mirror a long time
myself – a distant island

Cliff

At war's end, the women
pitched themselves off the top of
a cliff in Saipan oneafteranother

Out of virtue or duty or propriety
or something
Boxed in by fire, by men

They had to leap so they did
To the place you go when you've nowhere to go
(Cliffs always make a woman go head over heels)

And guess what
not one of them has reached the water yet
It's been fifteen years
what's going on
There, that
woman

Rakugo

In this world of ours
there's a man selling happiness and
a woman who sings 'Buy a dream'

In business novelty's the key
take it from me, kid, peddle suffering
and you'll make a mint
I'll buy that, says I, and
pile my old cart high
with everything from a heap
of family gravestones to my dead sister's love letters

Step right up, folks
what you see is what you get
any of it's a safer bet than stocks,
sadness doubles
tribulation does too
take this thick rope called kith and kin
twirl it once and a child's born
two twirls and hey, it's a grandkid!
Barely room for a body to perch
on this stone-stuffed cushion here
sit on it three years and your hair turns white,
do I have any takers?

The 'value' of money
the 'value' of possessions
the 'value' of a graduation diploma
why is it only things like that
that strut the streets in this part of town?

With all the smart-aleck yak about
Intangible Cultural Assets and the like hereabouts
why don't the value of poverty
the value of sighs
the value of souls bereft of ambition
fetch the highest prices?

Give me a family of six living in a single room and
I'll show you a fortune in tears, seven warehouses full

Think I exaggerate do you?
From a warehouse of tears I helped myself to
some little red bean-drops of blood
How about some of this   sweet bean soup?
At ten yen a bowl,
it hits the spot on a cold night like this,
folks

It don't appeal?
Then I'll have a sip myself and hey,
another

Festival of the Blind

Everyone has
two faces

One set of features
for the face above
and one for
the body below
(That set we're in
the habit of hiding)

The breasts are
sightless eyes,
and the blind know
even if you can't see things, they're there

Something must be there
touching makes it real
One day
in the joy and sadness of the thing made real
the woman's eyes brim over and
rain white tears

With white tears she'll raise a child

The small indentation in the middle of the belly
is a primeval nose,
the nose
in distant days within the womb
sniffed something strange
From there flower fragrance
tidal scent

wind and light blew in,
and those first memories
it tucked deep inside its own
soft folds

Below the nose
in women and men too lies a patch of grass,
and an ancient marsh ringed by ferns
insects chirping in their shade
many tongues burning

The tongues know,
about the feast soon to be arranged
on an oceanic table

Fruits which no country
has ever grown
splendid banquets
whose recipes no chef knows
wine of fire

All over the world
everyone flings off their clothes
sits down to table

Festival of the blind
bacchanal of drums
bonfires without heat without color

Seascape

The ocean isn't blue
it only looks blue

I'm a pure red ocean
only I don't look like an ocean

From birth
my whole body has been wrapped in skin
always quivering
with small waves
Lapping always lapping
against me
and all that surrounded me
against every shore

But no matter what
the rippling blood
couldn't separate from me and
move to the place called land

The surface of the skin for an instant
sun-warmed to body temperature
while the dark part within harbored
the depths of cold ancestral blood

Won't say more,
about what I am
except this
What I chewed up at table was rocks
what I spoke to in town was sand
what I embraced in the forest was the wind

I cover my face with my hands and
the fierce surging of waves begins,
it is sunset
darkness coming on
I become
an invisible woman

Kappa Heaven

And by the way, how's your job?
A gentle probe

'It weighs a lot, my pay'

    At least he had the decency not to ask
    if the weight came from its plenty

    Without it, I couldn't survive
    that's what weighs on me

    It comes in a flimsy beige-colored
    envelope made of paper, the only clothing I have
    to wrap around my life
    a bit like that scanty thing stuck to the kappa's back

    Leaving the spirit's unmentionable exposed for all to see
    and a made-up face thrown in for free

    Around here, everyone's a kappa
    so what's the difference

    (In fact we human beings may be living on the banks of
                      a story-book river somewhere)

I laughed cheerfully
and said
it's a wonderful place to work

That's how I answered the newspaper reporter who came
                                 one day from far away

The Runaway's Song

Home – a scab on the face of the earth
    A child with a boil keeps trying
    to pick off the crust
Home – a robe of golden brocade
    Even a packhorse driver's smart in tails
    An ugly girl decked out for the ball
Home – a flowerpot
    They dole out water and fertilizer and
    baby the buds
    Oh no, the root's outgrown the pot
Home – a pickling weight
    Please come out tasting like a fine human being
    Dear me, they've turned out sour
Home – a sweet little fort
    No one can wait
    to bring home the spoils
Home – a cradle of dreams
    In the cradle
    lives a praying mantis who dines on its mate
Home – a bank vault
    No meddling outsiders allowed in ever
Home – a grave every day
    And yet they say
    you can't come home again
    at the end
But even so everyone loves home
    Oh yes   love
Love – a scab
    A child with a boil..........

So come on everyone we're leaving home
let's go outside and lark around
abandon that wee little house
with its self-important lock
for the free and spacious fields

Nursery Rhyme

When Daddy died they laid
a white cloth on his face

Just like the white tea towel that's laid
on the food cooked for dinner

Everyone was crying
so I realized, Daddy must taste awful,
awful enough to make them cry

When Mama dies I'll do the laying
of the white cloth on her
she'll be like the three square meals they make us
eat every day

And when it's my turn to die
I'll do the best job of all
just you wait, I'll be like a gorgeous restaurant meal
beneath the white cloth

Fish and   chickens and   wild beasts
have such a yummy yummy way of dying

Sprouting

My house is small but the living is heavy
My two legs support it but
the roof is slowly caving in

Nothing for it but to
pluck out things like
hope and ideals and happiness one by one
those solid bone-like things
finally even pulling out
my backbone and then
my body collapses with a soft squish

In this house
chained to the past by the family altar,
the altar is the only lively part, so lively
it even has a kitchen
where cooking is done every day
May I survive those thick strong flavors
and blood-soaked calories
I pray, hands clasped, and then it happens

Octopus-like legs sprout
from my torso
four then five of them
then eight
What a relief now I'll be able to hold it up I think
and just then some strange human beings with vaguely
      familiar faces show up
come to eat the legs

Who are you?
I ask
your parents
they say
and tell me their names
have you forgotten?
they say

I shake my head weeping,
no
you're not my family
I'm an octopus, I'm not a human being

But human beings don't understand what
it's like for an octopus to have its eight legs eaten
yesterday one, today another
At the height of my misery
I tell all who will listen that
six of my legs were gnawed off,
but they retort
human beings are two-legged creatures from the get-go
and since you are one of them
there are certain things it's improper for you to say

That's what the family who loves me says
No matter how I pucker
or suck with my octopus lips
since true love
broad and deep
surrounds me like the ocean

surrounds me endlessly
from where I lost my legs
new legs will somehow sprout
as edible as always

from

My Life in Brief (1979)

略
歴

Ishigaki Rin, September 22, 1959, age 39. On the roof of the Industrial Bank of Japan, in her employee's uniform. Courtesy of Minamiizu-chō Public Library.

The Rite

It is good for a mother
to tie the strings of her white apron behind her
and step down to the wood-floored kitchen
and stand with her daughter before the sink

Over the washtub she lays
a fragrant new cutting board of wood
The teaching must begin from the
whole fresh fish
bonito or
sea bream
or flounder
will do
She places it on the board
then firmly grips a well-honed knife
and focusing all her force
in one stroke lops off its head
It is the mother's office
to pass on to her daughter when she becomes a woman
the feeling of those bones against the hand
and of the thick viscous blood

Before calling packaged chunks of meat 'ingredients'
and loftily discoursing on cooking as 'love'
How did we live
for all those long ages?
And how shall we live from here?

The Book of the Dead

It happened when my little sister was eighteen
and said she never wanted to grow up
I rushed to hide her in the grave

'Here I come'
'Not ready yet'

'Ready now?'
'No not yet'

Finally I burst out crying
And my sister cried herself to sleep inside the grave
How many years have passed since then

No one knows about our game of hide and seek
The day I disappear
will be the day I go to find my sister

'Ready or not, here I come'

Yesterday's Faces

Walked the mountains of Izu
the whole day
My face was bronzed so dark
by the sun
And yet the friend who went with me
didn't turn a shade darker

Remembered
the red flowers and
the white flowers
we saw in the mountains
That day
we bloomed too

Left
the dark face and
the pale face
in the mountains
Left quietly
without a word

Yesterday's faces that Izu's sun darkened
do not speak

They are looking toward me silently
from far away

My Life in Brief

I was born in a part of town that had a regimental headquarters

The barracks gate was well-defended
there were always sentries with bayonets standing in front
and soldiers in the guardhouse
searched everyone who came in
The barracks compound had a parade ground

I worked in a place with safe deposit boxes

The receptionist's job was to greet the customers warmly
and usher them in but
these days thirty years after the war
men dressed in security guards' uniforms
watch over the entrance like soldiers

The soldiers went to war

I reached retirement age and stopped working at the bank

When I walk around Marunouchi in Tokyo
I come across entrances policed by security guards
It makes me uneasy

I grew old in a part of town that had an Imperial palace

Tree

I went to that crematory for the first time in
a long while to say good-bye to an old friend

Forty years ago when she was four my little
sister turned to ashes in the same oven

That tree was standing in the garden
then too

Don't trees have eyes?
Or is it only that they keep them closed?

If so, when it opens its eyes
that tree will be amazed and say
What a terrible thing I've done
I've overlooked things of major importance

Such an old tree, I thought to myself
seeing it this time

It's stood by at the deaths
of so many people

You good-for-nothing
you're like me
just standing there not knowing the meaning of death

The tree murmured
Okay, maybe
when they carry you in I'll open my eyes

The Twilight Crane

It was
your first promise

In exchange for giving you
happiness and
love and
hope, that sort of thing –
that you would never look at me

You looked

Your nosiness
your greed
your limited intelligence

Now that you've seen me
I can't stay with you in the shape in which you saw me

Goodbye

When it was the crane in the story who said that
it was all right

The earth
is drifting away from human beings
It's getting
smaller and
small
er

Customs

These days
corpses have taken to wearing shoes

Of course
you can't go barefoot
on highways
or building sites
or in the darkness of mines

Once you're dead, you don't need to walk
They deliver you where you need to go
Because that's always been
the law of this land

The government doesn't observe the rules so
the shoe-wearing dead with their dun-colored faces
stagger to their feet
They wander in and out among the living

Sensing the hustle and bustle
even the ones who breathed their last in bed
want to wear shoes these days

After the Ceremony

With deepest reverence an aged mother receives her son's
decoration for soldiers who died in the war
A grown son's youthful hand grips his father's medal firmly

There the ceremony ended
After all the war's ended
More than twenty years have passed
Ending a ceremony is easy

Reality is not as easy
The soldiers who died with their eyes open
throng in belatedly, saying
oh, look
it's the great Empire of Japan
all the old familiar faces are here

How good to see you in such fine health, General
we are here at your service
There may not be another chance so please
hand out the medals to us in person

They're no use to our wives and children
Atten-shun!

Woman

And yet I still had faith
Even after the war was over
In the government offices
the public corporations
the banks
our country

In the upright character
of the public sector
That it was different
from a crooked landlord
a loan shark
or a conman

'I believed in you'
is all I say and
rise up
I've had enough,
oh what a fool I was

Lullaby

One day
one night
covered with a single layer of darkness she slept

Two days
two nights
beneath two sheets of night she dreamed

Ten days
a hundred nights a thousand quilts
blanketed the depths of sleep

Until the morning when the quilts
were peeled back and the earth spilled out

Good night good cheer
Good cheer good night

from

Tender Words (1984)

やさしい言葉

Ishigaki Rin, 1939, age 19.
Courtesy of Minamiizu-chō Public Library.

Sweetfish

Come on, we're going back upstream

Don't know where
to somewhere we
don't know

Something's flowing through the sky
in the old days soaked in light
Mom and Pop traced it
a river not on any map

Now the blood within me
commands me
says go home

Strange hometown
a place to finish something up for good

In early summer rapids
the shadow of a fish glimpsed for an instant
whose is
that slender finger?

Saying 'this way please'
it disappeared

Ishigaki Rin, 1937, age 17.
Courtesy of Minamiizu-chō Public Library.

Uncollected

Good Night

Good night

Night is rolling in
like the tide
Each of us floats in the sky
small islands above the earth

Every day
morning   noon   and evening
visit us from so far away
then leave and vanish into the distance

Like a thing that was plain for all to see
sometimes hides itself in the ocean
You get into bed
you sleep

Damp, sinking, forgetting ourselves

From the day   we were born
we have practiced how to sleep
Even so we can't always do it well

How are things going for you tonight?

With only a face   peeking out from the blankets
or keeping their head   under the covers
people   sleep
Here's to sweet dreams

In the deep darkness
that admits   no property rank or clothes
how tenderly, how warmly, how intensely
we all have lived

Deep night is visiting   the naked island
Close your eyes
Until tomorrow comes

Good night

Notes

Notes to the Poems

In these translations I have adhered to Ishigaki's somewhat idiosyncratic punctuation as closely as possible because it is intentional on her part and her guide for the reader.

GREETINGS
See pages 24–25 for Ishigaki's description of the poem's genesis.

AN EVENING TALE
On March 1, 1954, Japanese tuna fisherman aboard the fishing boat *Daigo Fukuryū Maru* (Lucky Dragon 5) were showered by nuclear fallout from the United States Castle Bravo thermonuclear weapon test at Bikini Atoll, Marshall Islands, one of 67 nuclear tests that the United States conducted on Bikini and Enewetak atolls from 1946 through 1958. The crew fell sick with acute radiation syndrome for some weeks and Kuboyama Aikichi, the boat's chief wireless operator, died of radiation sickness on September 23 of the same year. The American government did not admit full culpability but paid limited compensation to all the victims. This poem was written in 1954 and first published in the January 1955 issue of *Hiroba*, a magazine put out by the Education and Publicity Department of the Japanese Federation of Bank Employees' Unions.[1]

BEFORE ME THE SOUP POT THE RICE POT AND THE BRIGHT BURNING FLAME
First published in Ishigaki's workplace newspaper as part of a special issue devoted to women, this poem was later anthologized in *Poems by Bankers* (*Ginkō-in no shishū*, Japanese Federation

---

[1] Here and elsewhere information about date and place of first publication is from Takenaka Noriko and Nishihara Daisuke, 'Ishigaki Rin yonshishū shoshutsu ichiran,' *Hiroshima Daigaku Nihongo Kyōiku Kenkyū* 30, p. 9, http://doi.org/10.15027/49090

of Bank Employees' Unions, 1952), and then became the title poem of Ishigaki's first collection, published by Shoshi Yuriika in 1959.

IN A HUNDRED HUMAN BELLIES
In Japanese folklore the Princess of the Ocean is Otohime, the beautiful daughter of the Dragon King, who rules the oceans.

THE WOMEN'S BATH
Until late on the last day of the year, the typical working-class woman would clean and cook in preparation for the holidays and then go to the local public bath, with its large communal tubs, in order to be clean for the New Year. The gesture of modestly covering one's front is a typical sight in such venues. A freshly washed woman stepping out into the relatively clean and spacious dressing room might for a moment, thanks to the resemblance to the identical gesture of Botticelli's Venus, seem semi-divine. As Ishigaki wrote in reminiscing about the poem's inspiration:

> The women made their healthy bodies flush as they washed themselves clean in the soupy, grimy water. Cheap soap was the instrument of their purification, as if they were preparing for a ceremony on the morrow. As each woman came out of the bath having washed herself in those difficult conditions, I thought her beautiful. The pepper-and-salt perm describes exactly what I saw. The thought came, though it almost made me laugh at myself, that I was looking at the Venus of Japan. ('Onnayu,' *Sakoku*, 183–184)

THERE IS IN THIS WORLD
In 1999, this poem (first published in the workplace magazine *Ginkakei* in 1948) was used as the lyrics for one of the set piece

songs of the NHK (Japan Broadcasting Corporation) All-Japan School Choir Competition, a headline-making event.

ROOF
Tsubo: a traditional measure of area, equivalent to 3.31 square meters, or 35.58 square feet.

THESE DAYS I
The third stanza evokes the opening lines of the medieval epic *The Tale of the Heike*, 'The Jetavana Temple bells / ring the passing of all things [...] / The bold and brave perish in the end: / They are as dust before the wind.' (*The Tale of the Heike*, tr. Royall Tyler, Penguin, 2014)

The last stanza is reminiscent of Ki no Tomonori's poem in *One Poem Each by One Hundred Poets* (*Hyakunin isshu*): 'On a spring day / of peaceful overflowing / light / do the cherry blossoms scatter / with unquiet heart?' (tr. Janine Beichman).

These are spontaneous allusions to classical texts, rather than self-conscious literary ones. Ishigaki grew up at a time when educated people still referenced the classics in daily life, as the conversation with her grandfather quoted at the beginning of the Introduction suggests.

TRAVELING ON
'Autumn,' as a traveler through time, recalls the opening of Matsuo Bashō's travel diary *The Narrow Road to Oku (Oku no Hosomichi):* 'The months and days are the travellers of eternity. The years that come and go are also voyagers.' (*The Narrow Road to Oku*, tr. Donald Keene, Kodansha USA, 2017)

CLIFF
The Battle of Saipan, Northern Mariana Islands, which lasted from June 15 to July 9, 1944, was a decisive battle of the Pacific campaign, since it brought Japan within reach of United States B-29 bombers. In the wake of the Japanese defeat, when only

1,000 soldiers remained out of 31,000, there were thousands of civilian suicides (the exact number may never be known), including a large number of women who jumped off the island's cliffs, either out of fear of the enemy or because of military coercion by their own side, or both.

RAKUGO
Rakugo is the traditional art of the comic monologue, delivered by a single performer, who takes all the parts, kneeling on a cushion with nothing but a fan and a piece of cloth as props.

The second and third lines about the man and woman refer to popular songs of the 1950s that everyone knew: 'The Man who Sells Happiness' (*Kōfuku wo uru otoko*), translated from the French chanson 'Le Marchand de Bonheur,' and 'Buy a dream' (*Yume wo kaimashō*), a song composed for the ever-popular national Lottery (*takarakuji*).

'Sweet bean soup' is *shiruko*, a soup made of sweetened small red beans. Drinking it is a traditional winter pleasure.

KAPPA HEAVEN
Ishigaki's riff on 'Kappa Heaven' (*Kappa tengoku*), a much-loved manga series by Shimizu Kon, published in the *Asahi Weekly* 1953–1958, in which kappa were stand-ins for human beings, including office workers like Ishigaki's own colleagues.

In Japanese folklore, a *kappa*, 'river-child,' is a smallish amphibious creature who inhabits ponds and rivers. It is usually green, with webbed hands and feet and a turtle-like carapace on its back. It likes to bother human beings in various mischievous ways, though on occasion it is helpful.

THE RUNAWAY'S SONG
'Home': a translation of *ie*. The word signifies both a physical dwelling and the family who resides there. Combined with *seido*, system, as *ie seido*, it connotes the traditional extended family system, in which the patriarch held absolute authority.

'Boil': When Ishigaki was growing up and later in the postwar period, children frequently had boils. Malnutrition was so widespread that even slight cuts routinely became infected.

'Pickling weight': the stone or other heavy weight used to press down vegetables as they are cured; such pickled vegetables are a traditional staple of the Japanese diet.

THE BOOK OF THE DEAD
The title refers to the register that the lord of the underworld keeps of the dead.

THE TWILIGHT CRANE
The title refers to *The Twilight Crane*, a play by Kinoshita Junji based on a Japanese folk tale, which Ishigaki saw in 1986 ('Tobisaru,' *Taiko*, 140). A crane rewards the man who saved her life by secretly taking on the form of a woman, marrying him, and weaving beautiful cloth, which he then sells. Her only demand is that he not look at her at night while she weaves. The reason, unknown to him, is that she must revert to her animal form to weave the cloth, which is made from her own feathers. Goaded by greedy friends, he demands that she weave even more, and she does so, albeit reluctantly. But contrary to his promise never to watch as she weaves, he spies on her. With her secret discovered, she must return to the skies.

Ishigaki thought the most beautiful part of the performance was at the end, when the husband and his greedy friends, having discovered that the wife is missing, look up at the sky and admire a beautiful crane in flight. Even then, they do not realize what they have done.

GOOD NIGHT (*Oyasuminasai*)
This poem was commissioned by Tokai Television Broadcasting in 1980, to be recited to music and used as its sign-off when it went off the air at night. Once, while staying at a hotel in Tsu City, Mie Prefecture, Ishigaki turned on the television and

found herself being serenaded to sleep by it. (The anecdote as well as the poem's full text is in 'Matsuzaki,' *Taiko*, 181–182.) A number of viewers from Nagoya and environs still remember the sign-off fondly and have posted their recollections on the internet.

Original Poem Titles

from *Before Me the Soup Pot the Rice Pot and the Bright Burning Flame* 『私の前にある鍋とお釜と燃える火と』(1959)
- Greetings　「挨拶」
- An Evening Tale　「夜話」
- In a Hundred Human Bellies　「百人のお腹の中には」
- Before Me the Soup Pot the Rice Pot and the Bright Burning Flame　「私の前にある鍋とお釜と燃える火と」
- The Women's Bath　「女湯」
- There Is in This World　「この世の中にある」
- The Watcher　「それを見るのは」
- 0　「0」
- The Sea and Apples　「海とりんごと」
- Roof　「屋根」
- Poverty　「貧乏」
- The Pay Envelope　「月給袋」
- Getting Ready　「用意」
- These Days I　「私はこの頃」
- Secret　「ひめごと」
- This Overflowing Light　「この光あふれる中から」
- The Shoes That Fell Off　「ぬげた靴」

from *Nameplates and More* 『表札など』(1968)
- Little Clams　「シジミ」
- Nameplates　「表札」
- Living　「くらし」
- Traveling On　「旅情」
- Flowers　「花」

- Island 「島」
- Cliff 「崖」
- Rakugo 「落語」
- Festival of the Blind 「めくらの祭り」
- Seascape 「海のながめ」
- Kappa Heaven 「カッパ天国」
- The Runaway's Song 「家出のすすめ」
- Nursery Rhyme 「童謡」
- Sprouting 「生えてくる」

from *My Life in Brief* 『略歴』(1979)
- The Rite 「儀式」
- The Book of the Dead 「鬼籍」
- Yesterday's Faces 「きのうの顔」
- My Life in Brief 「略歴」
- Tree 「木」
- The Twilight Crane 「夕鶴」
- Customs 「風俗」
- After the Ceremony 「式のあとで」
- Woman 「女」
- Lullaby 「子守歌」

from *Tender Words* 『やさしい言葉』(1984)
- Sweetfish 「鮎」

Uncollected
- Goodnight 「おやすみなさい」

www.ingramcontent.com/pod-product-compliance
Lightning Source LLC
Chambersburg PA
CBHW020915090426
42736CB00008B/642